DEBT-FREE DREAMS:

STRATEGIES FOR PAYING OFF LOANS AND CREDIT CARDS

Emily-Rose Paulson

TABLE OF CONTENTS

Debt-Free Dreams:
Strategies for Paying Off Loans and Credit Cards

INTRODUCTION

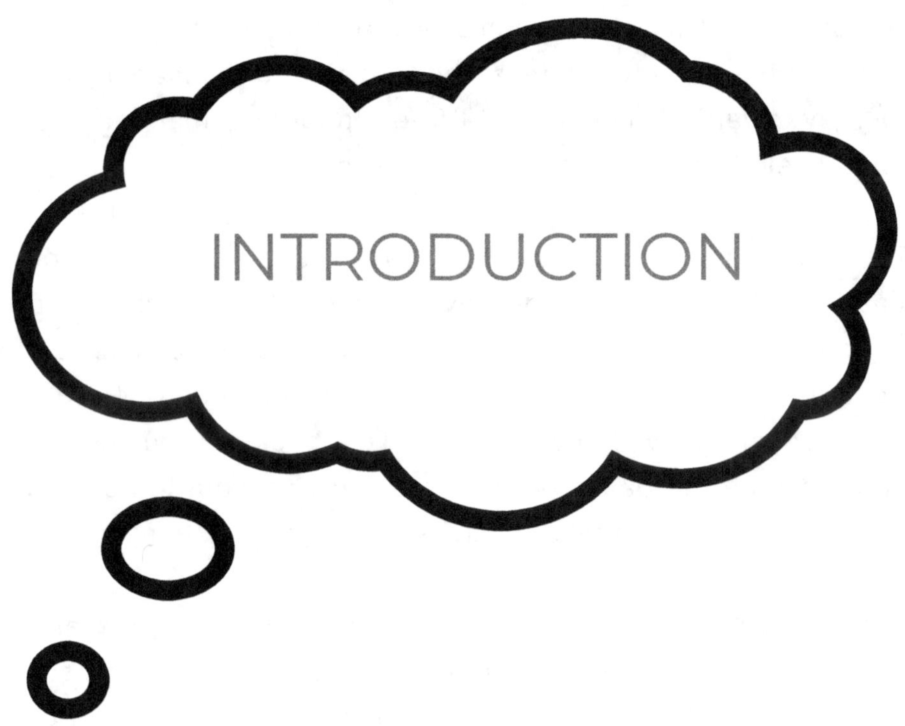

THE POWER OF FINANCIAL
FREEDOM THROUGH
DEBT-FREE LIVING

THE POWER OF FINANCIAL FREEDOM THROUGH DEBT-FREE LIVING

In a world driven by financial obligations and economic pressures, the concept of being debt-free has emerged as a beacon of hope and empowerment. Imagine a life unburdened by constant financial stress, where you have the ability to make choices based on your dreams and aspirations rather than the constraints of debt. This is the promise of embarking on a journey towards becoming debt-free – a journey that can lead to unparalleled financial freedom and peace of mind.

Debt, whether in the form of loans, credit cards, or other financial obligations, can quickly accumulate and cast a shadow over our lives. The weight of debt restricts our choices, limits our opportunities, and stifles our ability to achieve long-held goals. But it doesn't have to be this way. This book is a guide to help you navigate the path towards breaking free from the chains of debt, allowing you to take control of your financial destiny.

Why is becoming debt-free so important? The reasons are as diverse as the individuals who strive for this financial milestone. For some, it's the dream of homeownership, where a mortgage doesn't feel like a shackle but rather a stepping stone to stability. For others, it's the desire to launch a business venture unencumbered by the weight of loan repayments. And then some simply yearn for the peace of mind that comes from knowing their financial future is not dictated by creditors and interest rates.

Becoming debt-free isn't just about dollars and cents; it's about reclaiming control over your life. It's about charting a course towards a brighter and more liberated future, where your hard-earned money serves your dreams rather than perpetuating a cycle of indebtedness. It's about learning to manage your finances, make strategic decisions, and implement sustainable habits that will serve you well beyond your debt-free journey.

In this book, you will discover a range of strategies, insights, and actionable steps to help you conquer debt and achieve financial freedom. From creating a tailored debt repayment plan to adopting budgeting practices and exploring ways to increase your income, you'll find the tools you need to pave your way to a debt-free existence.

Remember, your journey towards becoming debt-free is a personal one, and every step you take is a step closer to your goals. So, dive into the following chapters with an open mind, a determined spirit, and the knowledge that pursuing a debt-free life is achievable and immensely rewarding. The path may have challenges, but the destination – a life unburdened by debt – is well worth the effort.

Let the adventure begin. Your financial freedom awaits.

UNDERSTANDING,
CALCULATING, AND
MANAGING DEBT

UNDERSTANDING, CALCULATING, AND MANAGING DEBT

Welcome to the first chapter of your journey towards financial freedom! In this chapter, we'll explore the world of loans and credit cards, equip you with the tools to calculate your debt and guide you through the process of creating a comprehensive debt inventory. By understanding your financial landscape, you'll be better prepared to take charge of your debt and work towards a debt-free future.

Quick Guide to Different Credit Cards and Loans

Navigating the world of credit cards and loans can be overwhelming, but understanding the basics can help you make informed financial decisions. Here's a quick guide to different types of credit cards and loans:

Credit Cards:

1. Standard Credit Cards:

These basic credit cards allow you to make purchases up to a specific credit limit. You need to pay back the amount you've spent, either in full by the due date or by making minimum payments, which accrue interest.

2. Rewards Credit Cards:

These cards offer rewards like cash back, travel points, or discounts when you make purchases. They can be beneficial if you pay off your balance in full each month to avoid high interest charges.

3. Balance Transfer Credit Cards:

These cards allow you to transfer balances from high-interest credit cards to a new card with a lower introductory interest rate. This can help you consolidate debt and save on interest.

4. Secured Credit Cards:

Geared toward building or rebuilding credit, these cards require a security deposit as collateral. They can be helpful if you have a limited or poor credit history.

5. Student Credit Cards:

Designed for students, these cards often have lower credit limits and may come with rewards tailored to student spending.

Loans:

1. Personal Loans:

Borrowed from a bank or lender, personal loans provide a lump sum you repay in fixed instalments over time. Interest rates can vary based on your credit score and other factors.

2. Mortgage Loans:

Used to buy homes, mortgage loans involve borrowing a large sum and repaying it over many years, with the home serving as collateral.

3. Auto Loans:

These loans help you buy a car. You borrow the money, make regular payments, and the car may serve as collateral.

4. Student Loans:

Specifically for education expenses, student loans can be federal or private. Repayment often begins after you graduate.

5. Home Equity Loans:

These loans let you borrow against the equity in your home. They can be helpful for major expenses like home improvements.

6. Payday Loans:

Short-term loans with high-interest rates are often due by your next paycheck. Be cautious due to their high fees.

Remember, the best financial decisions are based on your individual needs, goals, and circumstances. Before committing to any credit card or loan, research terms, interest rates, fees, and repayment plans. Always aim to borrow responsibly and make payments on time to maintain good financial health.

Calculating Your Total Debt and Interest Rates

Knowing the extent of your debt is crucial for crafting a strategic debt repayment plan. To begin, gather all your loan statements and credit card bills. Note down the outstanding balance for each and the respective interest rates. Summing up these amounts will give you a clearer picture of your total debt. Next, calculate the average interest rate by adding the individual rates and dividing by the number of debts. This average interest rate is a crucial metric for planning your repayment strategy.

Creating a Comprehensive Debt Inventory

Now, let's take the crucial step of creating a comprehensive debt inventory. This involves listing each of your debts, including personal loans, credit cards, and any other financial obligations. For each debt, record the following details:

Debt Inventory

1. Creditor/Lender:
Note the name of the bank, institution, or individual you owe money to.

2. Type of Debt:
Specify whether it's a personal loan, credit card, or other type of loan.

3. Outstanding Balance:
Write down the current amount you owe.

4. Interest Rate:
Record the interest rate associated with the debt.

5. Minimum Monthly Payment:
Note the minimum payment required each month.

6. Due Date:
Record the date the minimum payment is due.

7. Additional Notes:
Include any important information or terms related to the debt.

Creating a debt inventory gives you a bird's-eye view of your financial obligations. This step is crucial for visualizing the full scope of your debt and planning a repayment strategy that aligns with your financial goals.

As you move forward in this book, you'll learn about various strategies for repaying your debt, managing your finances, and ultimately achieving the freedom of debt-free living. Don't forget every step you take towards understanding and managing your debt brings you closer to regaining control of your financial future. Let's continue this journey together!

EXPLORING DEBT
REPAYMENT
STRATEGIES

EXPLORING DEBT REPAYMENT STRATEGIES

Regarding paying off debts, various strategies can help you efficiently achieve your debt-free goal. Two common approaches are the Snowball method and the Avalanche method. The Snowball method focuses on paying off your smallest debts first, while the Avalanche method prioritizes debts with the highest interest rates. By evaluating your financial circumstances, you can then customize a repayment plan that best suits your goals, lifestyle, and resources. This chapter will guide you through these strategies, offering insights into their advantages and helping you craft a plan tailored to your unique situation.

Here are some of the different debt repayment strategies that you can consider:

1. The Snowball Method:

Start by paying off the smallest debt first, regardless of the interest rate. Once the smallest debt is cleared, use the amount you were paying towards it for your next smallest debt, creating a "snowball" effect as you tackle more significant debts progressively.

2. The Avalanche Method:

Prioritize debts based on their interest rates. Focus on clearing the debt with the highest interest rate first, while making minimum payments on your other debts. Once the highest-interest debt is cleared, focus on the next highest debt and continue until all debts are paid off in full.

3. Debt Consolidation:

Merge multiple debts into a single loan or credit card with a lower interest rate. This can simplify your repayment plan and reduce overall interest payments. Be cautious about fees and terms associated with consolidation.

4. Debt Management Plan:

Enrol in a formal debt management program through a credit counselling agency. They negotiate with creditors to consolidate your payments into one monthly amount and potentially offer lower interest rates.

5. Bi-Weekly Payments:

Split your monthly payment in half and make payments every two weeks instead of once a month. This results in an extra annual payment and reduces the overall interest paid.

6. Increasing Minimum Payments:

Commit to paying more than the minimum required on your debts each month. This can help you pay off debts faster and save on interest.

7. Use Windfalls:

Apply any unexpected bonuses, tax refunds, or gifts towards your debt. This "found" money can substantially impact your repayment progress.

8. Debt "Snowflake" Strategy:

Whenever you come across small amounts of money (like from cashback rewards, garage sales, or selling unused items), use them to make extra payments towards your debts.

9. Balance Transfer:

High-interest credit card balances can be transferred to a new card with a lower introductory interest rate. This can help you save on interest while paying the principal faster.

10. Settlement Negotiation:

If you're struggling significantly, you might negotiate with creditors to settle your debt for a lump-sum payment that's lower than what you owe. Be mindful that this can negatively impact your credit score.

Remember, the effectiveness of these strategies depends on your financial situation, goals, and the types of debts you have. It's essential to carefully consider each strategy's pros and cons and how well it aligns with your repayment goals before implementing one.

CREATING A DEBT
REPAYMENT PLAN

CREATING A DEBT REPAYMENT PLAN

-17-

Creating a tailored debt repayment plan that aligns with your financial situation requires careful consideration and planning. Here's a step-by-step guide to help you craft a plan that suits your needs:

1. Assess Your Debt:

Start by gathering all your debt information. List each debt, including the type, outstanding balance, interest rate, and minimum monthly payment. This gives you a clear overview of your financial obligations.

2. Determine Your Budget:

Evaluate your monthly income and expenses. Calculate a realistic amount that you can afford to pay towards debt repayment without straining your essential living expenses. This will be the foundation of your repayment plan.

3. Choose a Repayment Strategy:

Consider the debt repayment strategies mentioned earlier, such as the Snowball method, Avalanche method, or other techniques that resonate with you. Your choice should match your financial goals, personality, and preferences.

4. Prioritize Debts:

If you opt for the Snowball method, order your debts from smallest to largest balance. If you choose the Avalanche method, prioritize debts with the highest interest rate. Alternatively, you can mix and match these strategies based on your comfort level.

5. Allocate Extra Funds:

Decide how much extra money you can put towards debt repayment each month. This could come from trimming unnecessary expenses, increasing your income, or reallocating windfalls like tax refunds or bonuses.

6. Set Realistic Goals:

Establish clear repayment milestones and goals. Define when you aim to pay off each debt and how much you intend to put towards them monthly. Make sure your goals are attainable within your budget.

7. Monitor progress:

Regularly track your progress against your goals. Celebrate small victories as you pay off debts, and adjust your plan if needed based on changes in your financial situation.

8. Stay Consistent:

Consistency is crucial. Stick to your plan even when challenges arise. Avoid incurring new debt while working on your repayment strategy.

9. Review and Adjust:

Periodically review your plan to see if it's still effective. If your financial situation changes, adjust your plan accordingly. Be flexible while maintaining your focus on becoming debt-free.

10. Seek Professional Help if Necessary:

If you find debt overwhelming, consider seeking advice from credit counselors or financial advisors. They can provide tailored guidance based on your specific situation.

Remember, a tailored debt repayment plan is about balancing aggressive repayment and maintaining a sustainable lifestyle. Customizing your plan ensures that it aligns with your unique financial circumstances, making your journey towards becoming debt-free both effective and manageable.

BUILDING A REALISTIC BUDGET: THE FOUNDATION FOR DEBT PAYOFF

BUILDING A REALISTIC BUDGET: THE FOUNDATION FOR DEBT PAYOFF

Welcome to Chapter 4, where we delve into the cornerstone of practical debt payoff—building a realistic budget. This essential step lays the groundwork for your journey to financial freedom. In this chapter, we'll explore the importance of budgeting in your debt payoff strategy, guide you through the process of identifying areas for potential savings, and provide insights on how to allocate funds towards your debt repayment goals.

4.1 The Importance of Budgeting in Debt Payoff

Budgeting is your compass in the sea of finances. It's the tool that helps you understand your income, expenses, and spending patterns. When it comes to debt payoff, a well-crafted budget provides a clear roadmap. It enables you to see exactly where your money is going and empowers you to make the right decisions about how much you can realistically allocate towards debt repayment.

4.2 Identifying Areas for Potential Savings

Analyze your spending habits to identify areas where you can cut back. Begin by categorizing your expenses into necessities (like housing, groceries, and utilities) and discretionary spending (like entertainment, dining out, and shopping). Explore potential savings by making conscious choices, like cooking at home instead of eating out or canceling subscriptions you no longer use.

4.3 Allocating Funds Towards Debt Repayment

Once you've created a clear picture of your income and expenses, it's time to allocate funds towards your debt repayment goals. Prioritize your debts based on your chosen repayment strategy. Determine how much extra money you can comfortably contribute to debt repayment each month without compromising your essential needs.

Creating a plan for allocating funds involves finding a balance between aggressively tackling debt and maintaining a manageable lifestyle. By striking this balance, you ensure your repayment plan is sustainable and aligned with your financial goals.

Remember, the purpose of building a budget is not to deprive yourself but to empower yourself. It's about making conscious choices that bring you closer to your debt-free destination. In the next chapter, we'll explore how to unleash your earning potential.

INCREASING YOUR INCOME: UNLEASHING YOUR EARNING POTENTIAL

INCREASING YOUR INCOME: UNLEASHING YOUR EARNING POTENTIAL

Welcome to Chapter 5, where we unlock the door to expanding your financial horizons—increasing your income. In this chapter, we'll dive into strategies that can help you bolster your earnings, accelerate your debt payoff journey, and pave the way to a debt-free future. From exploring side hustle opportunities to negotiating for a raise, we'll guide you through techniques that empower you to tap into your earning potential.

5.1 Exploring Side Hustle Opportunities

A side hustle is a powerful tool that allows you to leverage your skills and interests to generate additional income outside your primary job. The opportunities are vast, from freelance work and tutoring to selling products online or offering services. By dedicating your spare time to a side hustle, you can direct the earnings towards debt repayment, accelerating your progress and achieving your goals sooner.

5.2 Negotiating a Raise or Promotion

Advancing in your current job is a strategic move that can lead to a significant increase in income. Research industry standards and highlight your accomplishments when approaching your employer about a raise or promotion. Be prepared to showcase your value to the company and how your contributions have positively impacted their bottom line.

5.3 Using Your Skills to Generate Extra Income

Take a moment to identify skills you possess that could translate into additional income streams. If you're a skilled writer, consider freelancing. You might offer graphic design services if you have a knack for design. By monetizing your abilities, you can create new revenue streams that bolster your overall financial picture.

Increasing your income expedites debt repayment, expands your financial options, and increases your financial security. As you explore side hustles, negotiate for raises, and leverage your skills, you'll find yourself better equipped to conquer your debt while simultaneously advancing your financial future.

CUTTING EXPENSES AND SAVING MONEY: YOUR PATH TO FINANCIAL EFFICIENCY

CUTTING EXPENSES AND SAVING MONEY: YOUR PATH TO FINANCIAL EFFICIENCY

Welcome to Chapter 6, where we delve into the art of cutting expenses and saving money—a crucial step in your journey toward financial empowerment. In this chapter, we'll guide you through the process of analyzing your spending, making lifestyle changes to reduce costs, and uncovering practical ways to save on everyday expenses.

6.1 Analyzing Discretionary and Non-Discretionary Spending

Understanding your spending habits is vital to managing your finances. Start by categorizing your expenses into two main groups: discretionary and non-discretionary spending. Non-discretionary expenses are essential, like housing, utilities, and groceries. Discretionary expenses are extras, like dining out and entertainment. By separating these categories, you can identify areas where you have more control and can cut back.

6.2 Making Lifestyle Changes to Reduce Costs

Consider making minor adjustments to your lifestyle that can lead to significant savings over time. For instance, if you often eat out, try cooking more meals at home. If you're a fan of subscription services, evaluate which ones you can do without. By making conscious choices, you'll gradually reshape your spending habits and free up money for debt repayment.

6.3 Identifying Ways to Save on Everyday Expenses

Discovering ways to save on everyday expenses can make a big difference in your financial journey. Look for opportunities to save on things like groceries, transportation, and utilities. This could involve using coupons, carpooling, or negotiating better deals with service providers. Every little bit you save contributes to your overall financial well-being.

By optimizing your spending, you're taking control of your financial destiny. Cutting unnecessary expenses and adopting a frugal mindset not only accelerates your debt payoff but also cultivates a mindful approach to your finances.

NAVIGATING WITH CREDITORS AND LENDERS: THE ART OF FINANCIAL COMMUNICATION

NAVIGATING WITH CREDITORS AND LENDERS: THE ART OF FINANCIAL COMMUNICATION

Welcome to Chapter 7, where we focus on negotiating with creditors and lenders—a skill that can significantly impact your debt payoff journey. In this chapter, we'll guide you through the process of communicating with your creditors, including how to seek potential interest rate reductions, request payment plans or alternative arrangements, and master the art of negotiating for better terms.

7.1 Contacting Creditors for Potential Interest Rate Reduction

Initiating a dialogue with your creditors can open doors to potential interest rate reductions. Reach out to them, expressing your commitment to repaying your debt and inquiring about the possibility of lowering the interest rate. Presenting your case and demonstrating your determination can lead to revised terms that alleviate the financial burden.

7.2 Requesting Payment Plans or Alternative Arrangements

If your current payment structure is challenging, don't hesitate to discuss alternative arrangements with your creditors. Requesting a payment plan that aligns with your financial capacity or proposing an agreement to ease the burden can create a mutually beneficial solution. Communicating openly about your circumstances showcases your dedication to meeting your obligations.

7.3 The Art of Negotiating for Better Terms

Negotiating with creditors requires finesse. Gather your facts, outline your financial situation, and propose solutions that address your needs without jeopardizing your commitment to repayment. Approach the conversation with professionalism and remain open to compromise. Remember, creditors want to recover their money and are often willing to explore feasible solutions.

Effective negotiation enhances your repayment experience and strengthens your financial credibility. You can forge a collaborative relationship that benefits both parties by displaying your willingness to engage constructively.

In the subsequent chapter, we'll explore strategies to stay motivated and resilient as you navigate the intricate path of debt repayment.

STAYING MOTIVATED AND FOCUSED: NAVIGATING THE JOURNEY WITH RESILIENCE

STAYING MOTIVATED AND FOCUSED: NAVIGATING THE JOURNEY WITH RESILIENCE

Welcome to Chapter 8, a guide to keeping your spirits high and your focus unwavering throughout your debt repayment journey. In this chapter, we'll delve into strategies that help you celebrate small victories, bounce back from setbacks, and maintain the momentum needed to achieve your financial goals. We'll also explore the power of visualizing your debt-free future as a source of inspiration.

8.1 Celebrating Small Victories Along the Way

Acknowledging the progress you make, no matter how small, is crucial. Every debt payment is a step forward. Celebrate paying off individual debts or reaching milestones you set for yourself. Treating yourself to a small indulgence, sharing your achievements with a friend, or maintaining a progress journal can help you stay motivated and recognize your accomplishments.

8.2 Overcoming Setbacks and Maintaining Momentum

Setbacks are a natural part of any journey. Stay encouraged if you encounter unexpected expenses or challenges that hinder your progress. Reflect on your determination and remind yourself why you started this journey. Look for alternative solutions, adjust your plan, and maintain your momentum. Remember, setbacks don't define your journey—how you respond to them does.

8.3 Visualizing Your Debt-Free Future

Create a vivid mental picture of the life you'll lead once you're debt-free. Imagine the financial freedom, reduced stress, and opportunities that await. Visualizing your debt-free future keeps your goals in focus and inspires you to persist through tough times. You're working towards a brighter tomorrow; having this vision in mind can fuel your determination.

Maintaining motivation and focus is vital to overcoming challenges and achieving success. You'll remain steadfast on your journey toward financial freedom by celebrating your progress, maintaining resilience in the face of setbacks, and envisioning the debt-free life you're striving for.

BUILDING AND MAINTAINING
GOOD FINANCIAL HABITS:
NURTURING YOUR FINANCIAL
RESILIENCE

BUILDING AND MAINTAINING GOOD FINANCIAL HABITS: NURTURING YOUR FINANCIAL RESILIENCE

Welcome to Chapter 9, a deep dive into the world of cultivating strong financial habits. In this chapter, we'll explore practical ways to establish and uphold these habits, focusing on crucial aspects such as creating an emergency fund, gleaning wisdom from past financial missteps, and nurturing practices that shield you from future debt.

9.1 Establishing an Emergency Fund: Your Financial Safety Net

Imagine having a fund that stands ready to tackle unexpected financial curveballs. That's the beauty of an emergency fund. To build it, consider saving a small amount each month until it accumulates to three to six months' worth of living expenses. This fund is your go-to resource in times of crisis, helping you sidestep the need for credit cards or loans.

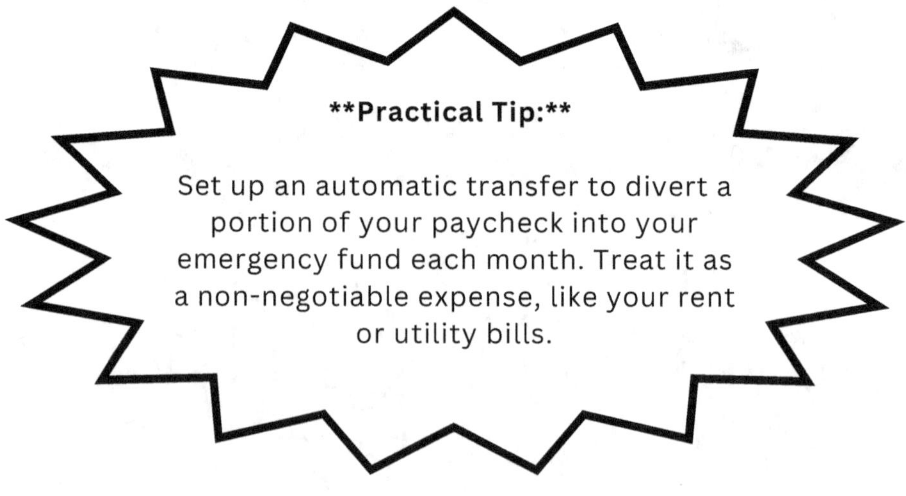

9.2 Learning from Past Financial Mistakes: Your Guide to Wiser Choices

Looking back on financial missteps is a step towards a brighter future. Identify instances where you overspent, mismanaged funds, or encountered debt. This introspection arms you with insights to dodge similar pitfalls in the future. For example, if credit card debt stems from impulsive purchases, adopt a habit of giving yourself a cooling-off period before making non-essential buys.

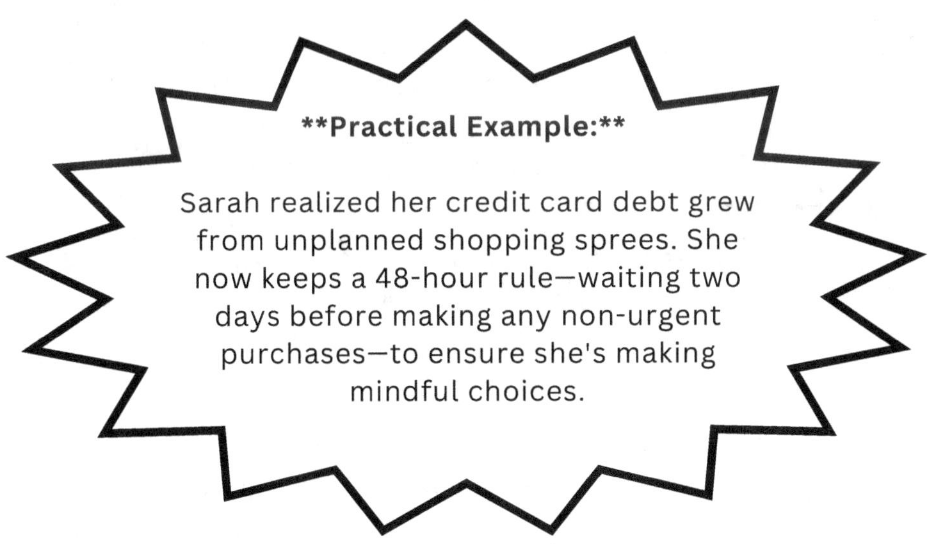

9.3 Cultivating Habits to Prevent Future Debt: A Blueprint for Financial Strength

Preventing future debt is rooted in forming robust financial habits. Embrace practices like tracking your spending, living within your means, and regular budget reviews. Strengthen your resolve to differentiate between needs and wants. For instance, consider cooking more meals at home instead of dining out frequently.

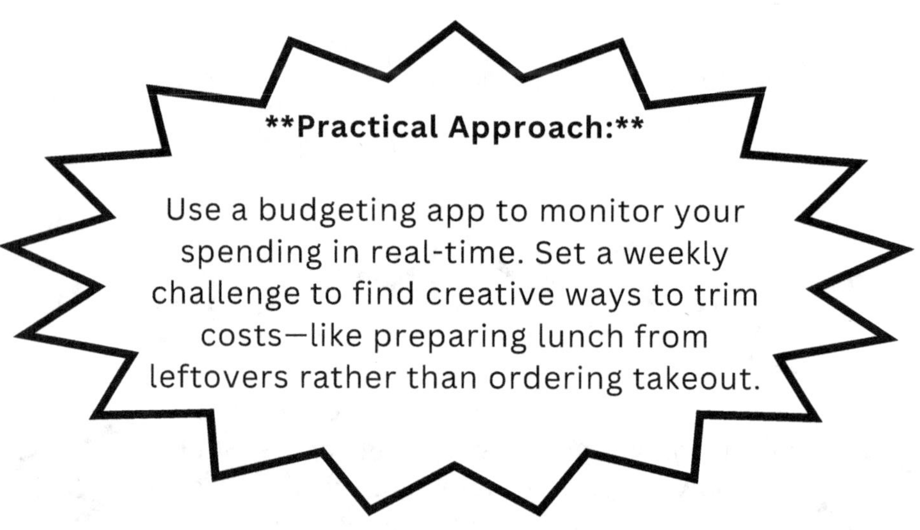

By integrating these practices into your daily life, you're nurturing the foundation of a secure financial future. As we wrap up, we'll discuss the transition to a debt-free life and the boundless opportunities that await you on the other side.

EXPLORING DEBT CONSOLIDATION AND REFINANCING: NAVIGATING YOUR FINANCIAL OPTIONS

EXPLORING DEBT CONSOLIDATION AND REFINANCING: NAVIGATING YOUR FINANCIAL OPTIONS

Welcome to Chapter 10, where we embark on a journey through the realm of debt consolidation and refinancing—two strategies that can potentially reshape your financial landscape. In this chapter, we'll examine the pros and cons of debt consolidation loans, explore refinancing options for credit card debt, and guide you on when and how to consider these strategies.

10.1 Pros and Cons of Debt Consolidation Loans: The Big Picture

Debt consolidation loans offer a chance to merge multiple debts into a single loan with a potentially lower interest rate. The benefits are evident: simplified payments and potential savings on interest. However, it's crucial to weigh the advantages against potential drawbacks. While monthly payments might be more manageable, you could pay more interest over the long term if the loan term is extended.

10.2 Refinancing Options for Credit Card Debt: Rethinking Your Approach

Refinancing credit card debt involves transferring high-interest balances to a lower-interest account. This can lead to substantial interest savings, making it easier to pay off your debt faster. Balance transfer cards and personal loans are standard refinancing options. However, be wary of transfer fees and ensure discipline in avoiding accumulating new debt.

10.3 When and How to Consider These Strategies: Guiding Factors

Debt consolidation and refinancing aren't one-size-fits-all solutions. Consider them when you have a clear plan to manage your spending and avoid incurring new debt. Evaluate your credit score, compare interest rates, and calculate the potential savings. Ensure the monthly payments and terms align with your financial situation and goals.

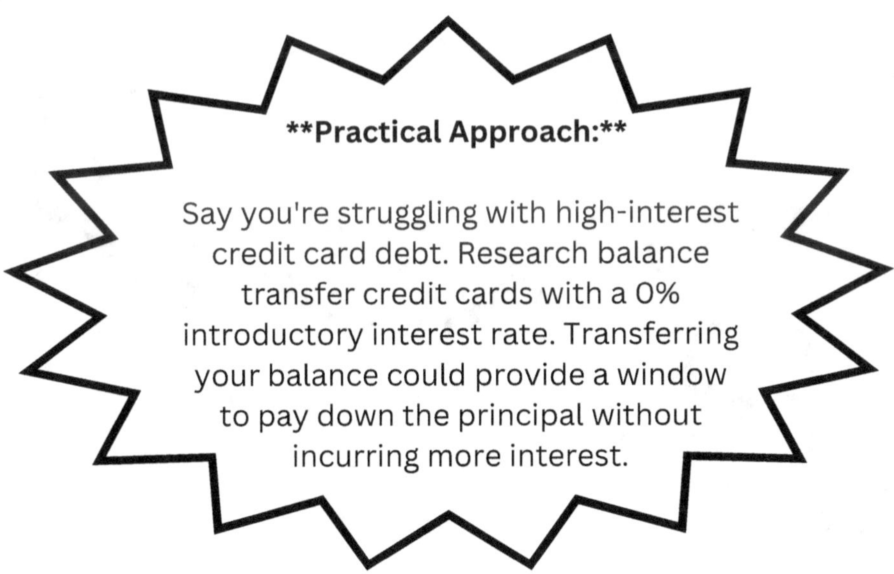

Remember, debt consolidation and refinancing are tools that can aid your journey to financial freedom, but they're most effective when combined with disciplined financial practices.

NAVIGATING FINANCIAL
SETBACKS: OVERCOMING
CHALLENGES WITH RESILIENCE

NAVIGATING FINANCIAL SETBACKS: OVERCOMING CHALLENGES WITH RESILIENCE

-43-

Welcome to Chapter 11, a guide to navigating the inevitable bumps on your financial journey. In this chapter, we'll explore practical ways to handle unexpected expenses, adapt your debt repayment plan when necessary, and employ strategies to stay on course during challenging times.

11.1 Dealing with Unexpected Expenses: Tackling Financial Surprises

Life is filled with surprises, some of which come with price tags. These unexpected expenses can derail your financial progress, whether it's a medical bill, car repair, or unforeseen event. Create an emergency fund as a buffer against such scenarios, and if necessary, tap into it to avoid resorting to high-interest credit options.

11.2 Adjusting Your Debt Repayment Plan When Necessary: Flexibility in Action

Financial setbacks may call for adjustments to your debt repayment plan. If you're facing reduced income or increased expenses, revisit your budget to see where you can temporarily trim costs. If necessary, contact creditors to discuss modified payment plans or hardship programs. Staying adaptable is critical to maintaining control during challenges.

11.3 Strategies for Staying on Track During Challenging Times: Resilience in Practice

Staying on track when facing financial difficulties requires resilience and resourcefulness. Stay connected to your goals, and remember why you started your debt repayment journey. Seek support from friends, family, or financial counselors who can offer guidance. Maintain open communication with creditors if you encounter difficulties in meeting payments.

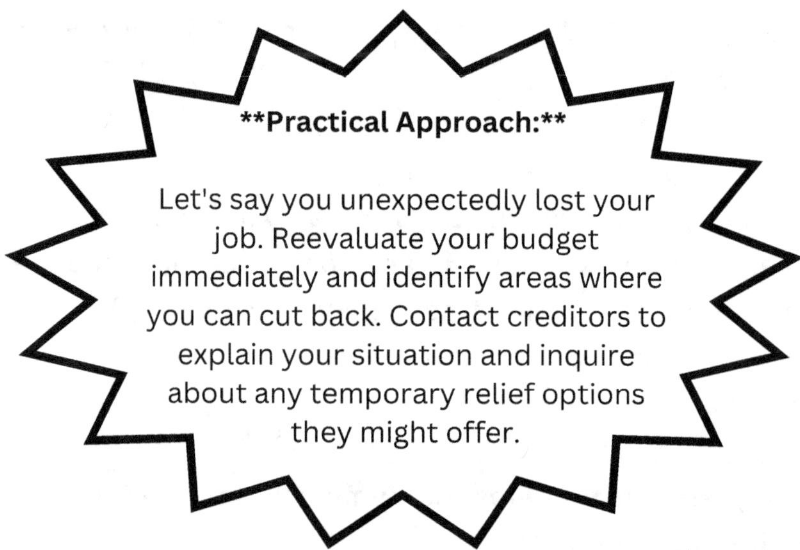

Remember, setbacks don't define your journey—they're temporary hurdles that perseverance can overcome. By handling unexpected expenses with preparedness, adapting your plan when needed, and employing strategies to remain steadfast, you demonstrate your commitment to achieving financial freedom. In our final chapter, we'll reflect on your debt repayment journey and prepare for the bright road ahead.

CELEBRATING YOUR DEBT-FREE SUCCESS: EMBRACING A NEW BEGINNING

CELEBRATING YOUR DEBT-FREE SUCCESS: EMBRACING A NEW BEGINNING

Welcome to Chapter 12, the culmination of your remarkable journey towards financial liberation. In this final chapter, we'll celebrate your achievement of becoming debt-free, reflect on the path you've traveled, and lay the groundwork for a future filled with newfound possibilities.

12.1 Reaching Your Debt-Free Goal: A Triumph of Determination

Congratulations are in order! You've conquered the challenges, embraced discipline, and worked diligently to free yourself from the burden of debt. Your journey is a testament to your determination and commitment to shaping your financial destiny.

12.2 Reflecting on Your Journey to Financial Freedom: Lessons Learned

Take a moment to reflect on your journey. Consider the financial habits you've cultivated, the resilience you've shown in the face of setbacks, and the milestones you've achieved. Reflect on the valuable lessons you've learned about managing money, making informed decisions, and staying dedicated to your goals.

12.3 Planning for a Debt-Free Future: Unleashing New Possibilities

As you stand on the threshold of a debt-free future, look ahead with optimism. Your financial freedom is the foundation for a life rich in possibilities. Set new goals, whether they involve building savings, investing, or pursuing dreams that were once on hold. Use your acquired skills to make informed financial choices and continue your journey towards prosperity.

Your journey to becoming debt-free is more than a financial accomplishment—it's a transformation that impacts every facet of your life. As you celebrate this achievement, remember that financial freedom is an ongoing journey. By staying vigilant, nurturing healthy financial habits, and embracing opportunities, you're paving the way to a life of empowerment, security, and unlimited potential. Congratulations on reaching this significant milestone!

EMBRACING FINANCIAL
INDEPENDENCE

EMBRACING FINANCIAL INDEPENDENCE

In the pages of this journey, you've embarked on a transformative adventure that has empowered you to take control of your finances, conquer debt, and pave the way for a brighter future. The strategies, insights, and practices you've absorbed are not just tools but the keys to unlocking a life of financial independence and boundless possibilities.

Remember that your debt-free journey is not just about numbers—it's about reclaiming your peace of mind, reducing stress, and gaining the freedom to pursue your dreams. Your path requires dedication, discipline, and willingness to face challenges head-on. You've achieved a debt-free status and cultivated the skills needed to navigate your financial terrain with wisdom.

As you move forward, continue to apply the strategies you've learned. Stay vigilant about your spending, be adaptable in the face of setbacks, and keep nurturing your financial knowledge. Your journey doesn't end here; it transforms into a life lived on your terms, unburdened by debt and fueled by empowerment.

As you bask in the glow of your accomplishment, remember that your story has the power to inspire others. Share your journey, your successes, and the lessons you've learned. Please encourage others to embark on their own debt-free journeys, guiding them towards the freedom and autonomy you've achieved.

Thank you for entrusting this journey to guide you towards financial independence. May your debt-free journey continue to shine as an inspiration and a testament to the remarkable impact of determination, commitment, and financial empowerment.

Budget
Plans

Budget
Plans

Budget
Plans

Budget
Plans

Budget
Plans

Budget
Plans

Budget
Plans

Budget
Plans

Budget
Plans

Budget
Plans

Budget
Plans

Budget
Plans

Budget
Plans

Budget
Plans

Budget
Plans

Budget
Plans

Budget
Plans

Budget
Plans

Budget
Plans

Budget
Plans

Budget
Plans

Budget
Plans

Budget
Plans

Budget
Plans

Budget
Plans

Budget
Plans